USA

FACT BOOK

CHRISTOPHER L. HICKMAN

1st WORLD
PUBLISHING

USA FACTBOOK

CHRISTOPHER L. HICKMAN

© Christopher L. Hickman 2005

Published by 1stWorld Publishing
1100 North 4th St. Suite 131, Fairfield, Iowa 52556
tel: 641-209-5000 • fax: 641-209-3001
web: www.1stworldpublishing.com

First Edition

LCCN: 2005935504
SoftCover ISBN: 1-59540-969-6
HardCover ISBN: 1-59540-971-8
eBook ISBN: 1-59540-970-X

TABLE OF CONTENTS

THE STATES

1. ALABAMA

Date - 12-14-1819 (#22)
Capital - Montgomery
Nickname - Yellowhammer State
Flower - Camellia
Bird - Yellowhammer
Song - Alabama

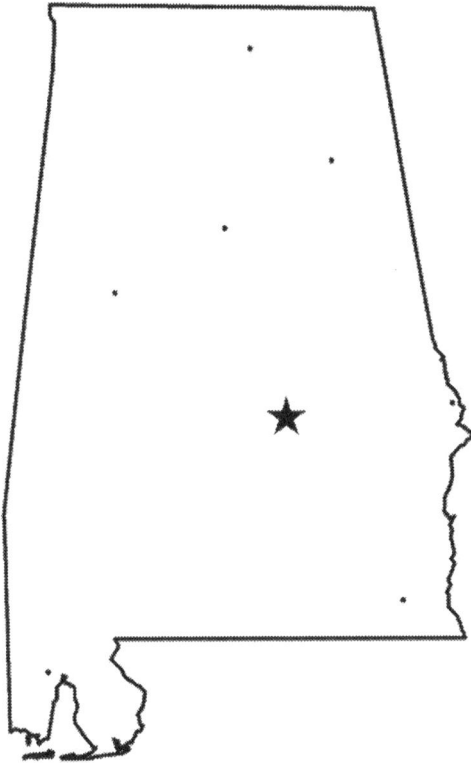

2. ALASKA

Date - 1-3-1959 (#49)
Capital - Juneau
Nickname - The Last Frontier
Flower - Forget Me Not
Bird - Willow Ptarmigan
Song - Alaska's Flag

3. ARIZONA

Date - 2-14-1912 (#48)
Capital - Phoenix
Nickname - Grand Canyon State
Flower - Saguaro Cactus Blossom
Bird - Cactus Wren
Song - Arizona

USA FACTBOOK

4. ARKANSAS

Date - 6-15-1836 (#25)
Capital - Little Rock
Nickname - The Natural State
Flower - Apple Blossom
Bird - Mockingbird
Song - 1. Arkansas   2. Oh, Arkansas

USA FACTBOOK

5. CALIFORNIA

Date - 9-9-1850 (#31)
Capital - Sacramento
Nickname - The Golden State
Flower - California Poppy
Bird - California Valley Quail
Song - I Love You, California

6. COLORADO

Date - 8-1-1876 (#38)
Capital - Denver
Nickname - The Centennial State
Flower - Rocky Mountain Columbine
Bird - Lark Bunting
Song - Where the Columbines Grow

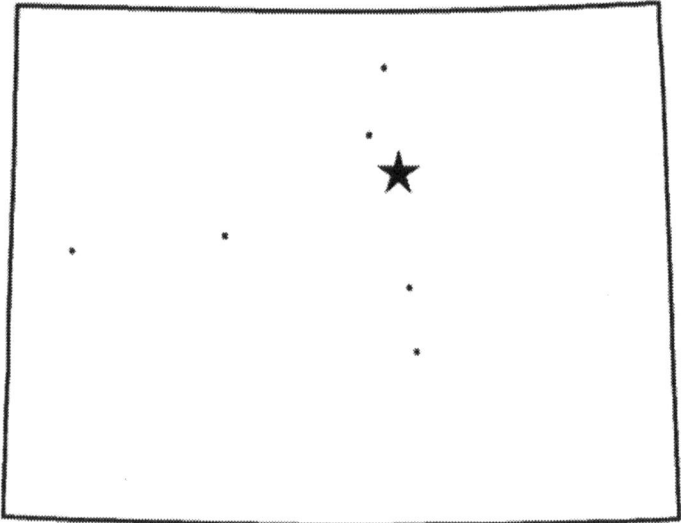

7. CONNECTICUT

Date - 1-9-1788 (#5)
Capital - Hartford
Nickname - The Constitution State
Flower - Mountain Laurel
Bird - Robin
Song - Yankee Doodle

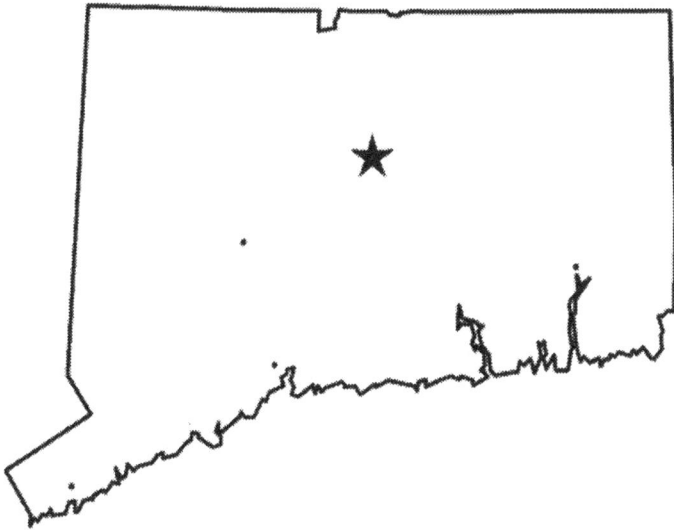

8. DELAWARE

Date - 12-7-1787 (#1)
Capital - Dover
Nickname - The First State
Flower - Peach Blossom
Bird - Blue Hen Chicken
Song - Our Delaware

9. FLORIDA

Date - 3-3-1845 (#27)
Capital - Tallahassee
Nickname - The Sunshine State
Flower - Orange Blossom
Bird - Mockingbird
Song - 1. Swanee River 2. Florida, My Florida

10. GEORGIA

Date - 1-2-1788 (#4)
Capital - Atlanta
Nickname - The Peach State
Flower - Cherokee Rose
Bird - Brown Thrasher
Song - Georgia on my Mind

11. HAWAII

Date - 8-21-1959 (#50)
Capital - Honolulu
Nickname - The Aloha State
Flower - Pau Aloalo
Bird - Nene
Song - Hawaii Ponoi

12. IDAHO

Date - 7-3-1890 (#43)
Capital - Boise
Nickname - The Gem State
Flower - Syringa - Mock Orange
Bird - Mountain Bluebird
Song - Here We Have Idaho

USA FACTBOOK

13. ILLINOIS

Date - 12-3-1818 (#21)
Capital - Springfield
Nickname - The Prairie State
Flower - Purple Violet
Bird - Cardinal
Song - Illinois

14. INDIANA

Date - 12-11-1816 (#19)
Capital - Indianapolis
Nickname - The Hoosier State
Flower - Peony
Bird - Cardinal
Song - On the Banks of the Wabash

USA FACTBOOK

15. IOWA

Date - 12-28-1846 (#29)
Capital - Des Moines
Nickname - The Hawkeye State
Flower - Wild Prairie Rose
Bird - Eastern Goldfinch
Song - The Song of Iowa

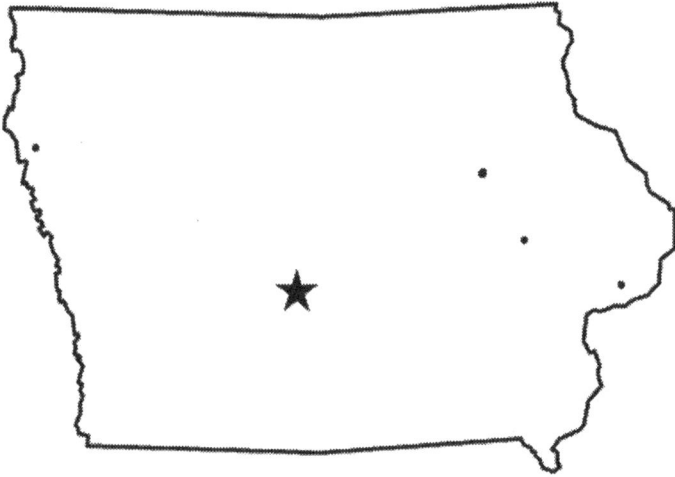

16. KANSAS

Date - 1-29-1861 (#34)
Capital - Topeka
Nickname - The Sunflower State
Flower - Sunflower
Bird - Western Meadowlark
Song - Home on the Range

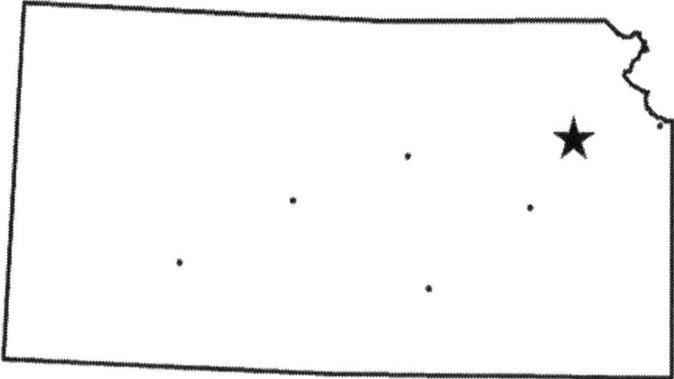

17. KENTUCKY

Date - 6-1-1792 (#15)
Capital - Frankfort
Nickname - The Bluegrass State
Flower - Goldenrod
Bird - Cardinal
Song - My Old Kentucky Home

18. LOUISIANA

Date - 4-30-1812 (#18)
Capital - Baton Rouge
Nickname - The Pelican State
Flower - Magnolia
Bird - Eastern Brown Pelican
Song - 1. Give Me Louisiana 2. You Are My Sunshine

19. MAINE

Date - 3-15-1820 (#23)
Capital - Augusta
Nickname - The Pine Tree State
Flower - White Pine Cone and Tassel
Bird - Chickadee
Song - State Song of Maine

20. MARYLAND

Date - 4-28-1788 (#7)
Capital - Annapolis
Nickname - The Old Line State
Flower - Black-eyed Susan
Bird - Baltimore Oriole
Song - Maryland, My Maryland

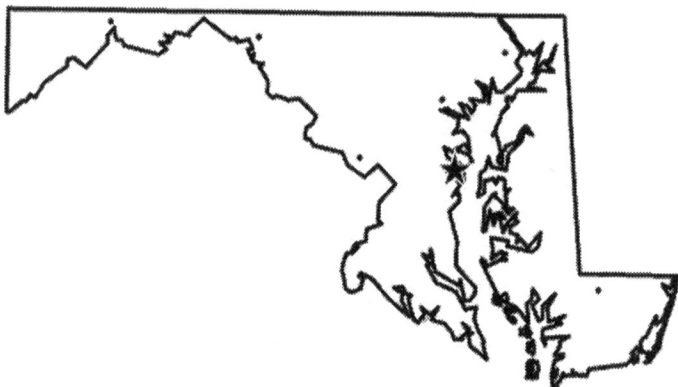

21. MASSACHUSETTS

Date - 2-6-1788 (#6)
Capital - Boston
Nickname - The Bay State
Flower - Mayflower
Bird - Chickadee
Song - Hail Massachusetts

22. MICHIGAN

Date - 1-26-1837 (#26)
Capital - Lansing
Nickname - The Great Lakes State
Flower - Apple Blossom
Bird - Robin
Song - Michigan, My Michigan

23. MINNESOTA

Date - 5-11-1858 (#32)
Capital - St. Paul
Nickname - The North Star State
Flower - Pink and White Lady's-slipper
Bird - Common Loon
Song - Hail Minnesota

24. MISSISSIPPI

Date - 12-10-1817 (#20)
Capital - Jackson
Nickname - The Magnolia State
Flower - Magnolia
Bird - Mockingbird
Song - Go Mis-sis-sip-pi

25. MISSOURI

Date - 8-10-1821 (#24)
Capital - Jefferson City
Nickname - The Show Me State
Flower - Hawthorn
Bird - Bluebird
Song - Missouri Waltz

26. MONTANA

Date - 11-8-1889 (#41)
Capital - Helena
Nickname - The Treasure State
Flower - Bitterroot
Bird - Western Meadowlark
Song - 1. Montana 2. Montana Melody

27. NEBRASKA

Date - 3-1-1867 (#37)
Capital - Lincoln
Nickname - The Cornhusker State
Flower - Goldenrod
Bird - Western Meadowlark
Song - Beautiful Nebraska

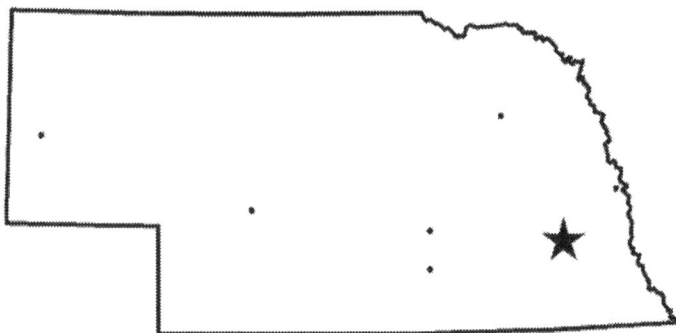

28. NEVADA

Date - 10-31-1864 (#36)
Capital - Carson City
Nickname - The Silver State
Flower - Sagebrush
Bird - Mountain Bluebird
Song - Home Means Nevada

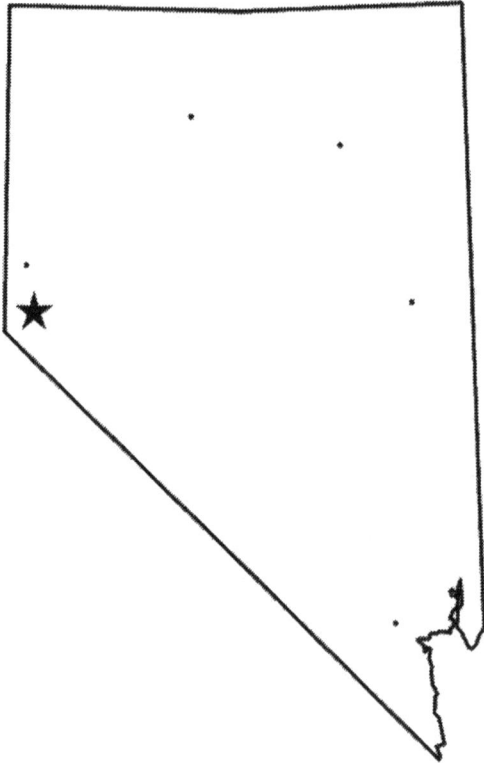

USA FACTBOOK

29. NEW HAMPSHIRE

Date - 6-21-1788 (#9)
Capital - Concord
Nickname - The Granite State
Flower - Purple Lilac
Bird - Purple Finch
Song - Old New Hampshire

30. NEW JERSEY

Date - 12-18-1787 (#3)
Capital - Trenton
Nickname - The Garden State
Flower - Violet
Bird - Eastern Goldfinch
Song - I'm From New Jersey

31. NEW MEXICO

Date - 1-6-1912 (#47)
Capital - Sante Fe
Nickname - The Land of Enchantment
Flower - Yucca Flower
Bird - Roadrunner
Song - O, Fair New Mexico

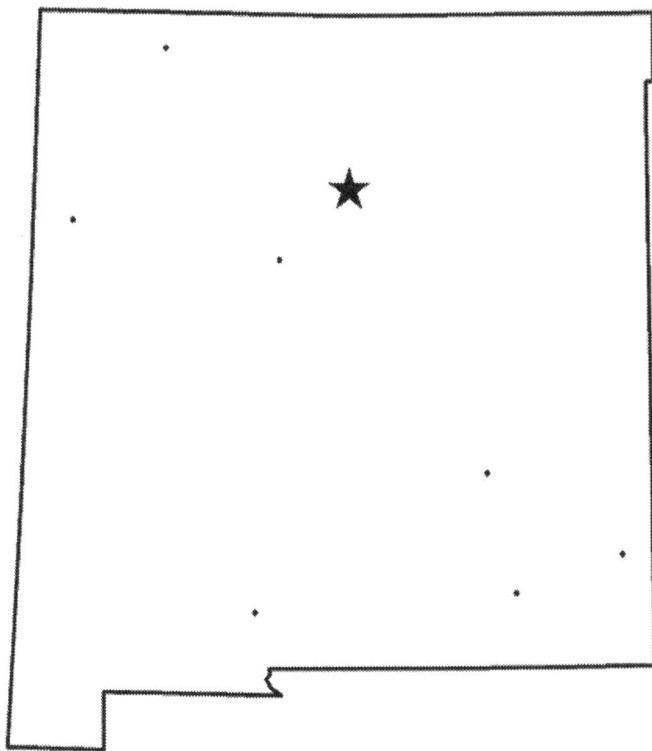

32. NEW YORK

Date - 7-26-1788 (#11)
Capital - Albany
Nickname - The Empire State
Flower - Rose
Bird - Bluebird
Song - I love New York

33. NORTH CAROLINA

Date - 11-21-1789 (#12)
Capital - Raleigh
Nickname - The Tar Heel State
Flower - American Dogwood
Bird - Cardinal
Song - The Old North State

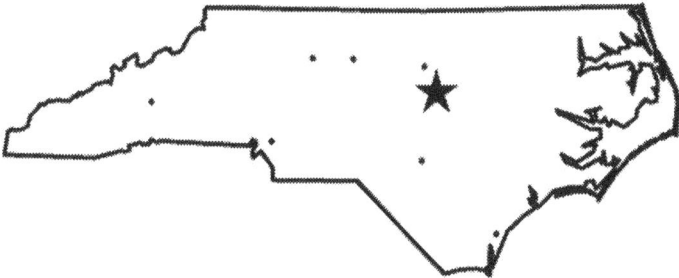

34. NORTH DAKOTA

Date - 11-2-1889 (#39 or #40)
Capital - Bismark
Nickname - The Peace Garden State
Flower - Wild Prairie Rose
Bird - Western Meadowlark
Song - North Dakota Hymn

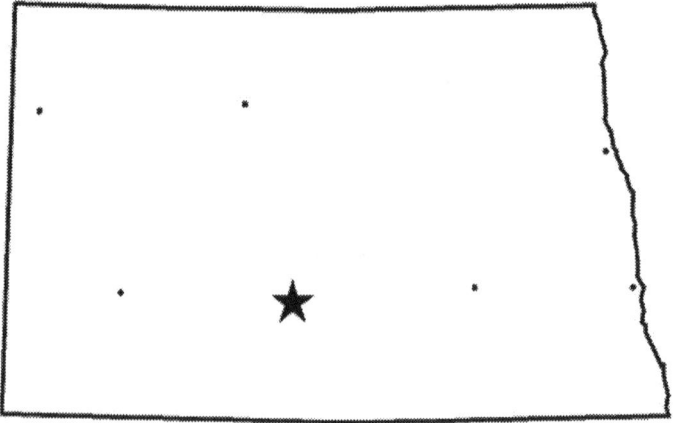

35. OHIO

Date - 3-1-1803 (#17)
Capital - Columbus
Nickname - The Buckeye State
Flower - Scarlet Carnation
Bird - Cardinal
Song - Beautiful Ohio

USA FACTBOOK

36. OKLAHOMA

Date - 11-16-1907 (#46)
Capital - Oklahoma City
Nickname - The Sooner State
Flower - Mistletoe
Bird - Scissor-tailed Flycatcher
Song - Oklahoma

37. OREGON

Date - 2-14-1859 (#33)
Capital - Salem
Nickname - The Beaver State
Flower - Oregon Grape
Bird - Western Meadowlark
Song - Oregon, My Oregon

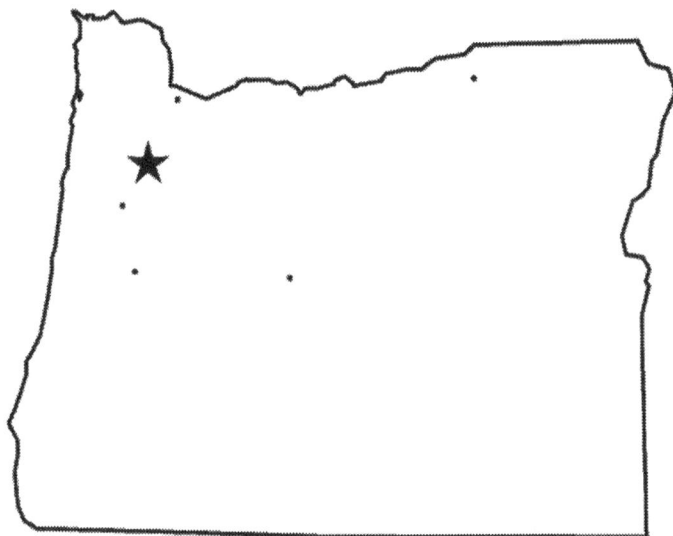

38. PENNSYLVANIA

Date - 12-12-1787 (#2)
Capital - Harrisburg
Nickname - The Keystone State
Flower - Mountain Laurel
Bird - Ruffed Grouse
Song - Pennsylvania

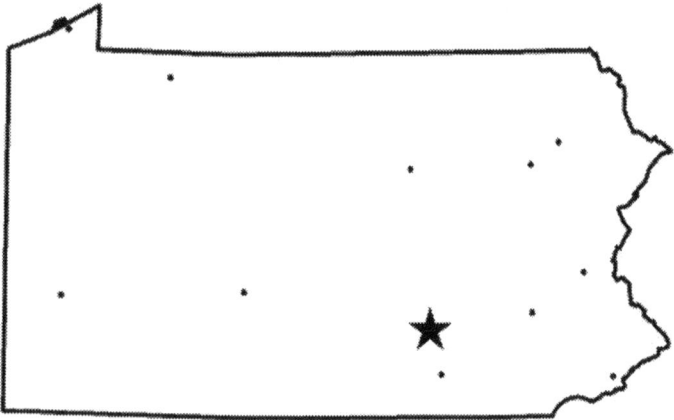

USA FACTBOOK

39. RHODE ISLAND

Date - 5-29-1790 (#13)
Capital - Providence
Nickname - The Ocean State
Flower - Violet
Bird - Rhode Island Red
Song - Rhode Island, It's for me

40. SOUTH CAROLINA

Date - 5-23-1788 (#8)
Capital - Columbia
Nickname - The Palmetto State
Flower - Yellow Jessamine
Bird - Great Carolina Wren
Song - Carolina

41. SOUTH DAKOTA

Date - 11-2-1889 (#39 or #40)
Capital - Pierre
Nickname - Mount Rushmore State
Flower - Pasque Flower
Bird - Ring-necked Pheasant
Song - Hail South Dakota

42. TENNESSEE

Date - 6-1-1796 (#16)
Capital - Nashville
Nickname - The Volunteer State
Flower - Iris
Bird - Mockingbird
Song - 1. Tennessee 2. My Tennessee 3. Rock
Top 4. My Homeland Tennessee 5. When It's
Iris Time in Tennessee 6. The Tennessee Waltz

43. TEXAS

Date - 12-29-1845 (#28)
Capital - Austin
Nickname - The Lone Star State
Flower - Bluebonnet
Bird - Mockingbird
Song - Texas, Our Texas

44. UTAH

Date - 1-4-1896 (#45)
Capital - Salt Lake City
Nickname - The Beehive State
Flower - Sego Lily
Bird - California Seagull
Song - Utah, We Love Thee

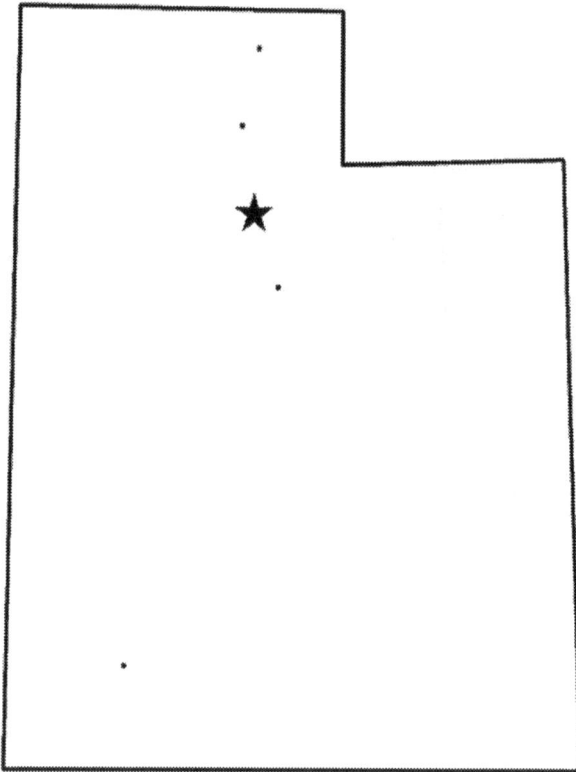

45. VERMONT

Date - 3-4-1791 (#14)
Capital - Montpelier
Nickname - The Green Mountain State
Flower - Red Clover
Bird - Hermit Thrush
Song - Hail Vermont

46. VIRGINIA

Date - 6-25-1788 (#10)
Capital - Richmond
Nickname - The Old Dominion State
Flower - American Dogwood
Bird - Cardinal
Song - Carry Me Back to Old Virginia

47. WASHINGTON

Date - 11-11-1889 (#42)
Capital - Olympia
Nickname - The Evergreen State
Flower - Pink Rhododendron
Bird - Willow Goldfinch
Song - Washington, My Home

48. WEST VIRGINIA

Date - 6-20-1863 (#35)
Capital - Charleston
Nickname - The Mountain State
Flower - Rhododendron
Bird - Cardinal
Song - West Virginia Hills

49. WISCONSIN

Date - 5-29-1848 (#30)
Capital - Madison
Nickname - The Badger State
Flower - Wood Violet
Bird - Robin
Song - On Wisconsin

USA FACTBOOK

50. WYOMING

Date - 7-10-1890 (#44)
Capital - Cheyenne
Nickname - The Equality State
Flower - Indian Paintbrush
Bird - Western Meadowlark
Song - Wyoming

THE PRESIDENTS

1. George Washington

Born - 2-22-1732
Died - 12-14-1799
Place of Birth - Pope's Creek, Virginia
Vice President - John Adams
Term in Office - 4-30-1789 to 3-3-1797
Political Party - Federalist

2. JOHN ADAMS

Born - 10-30-1735
Died - 7-4-1826
Place of Birth - Braintree, Massachusetts
Vice President - Thomas Jefferson
Term in Office - 3-4-1797 to 3-3-1801
Political Party - Federalist

3. Thomas Jefferson

Born - 4-13-1743
Died - 7-4-1826
Place of Birth - Shadwell, Virginia
Vice Presidents - Aaron Burr, George Clinton
Term in Office - 3-4-1801 to 3-3-1809
Political Party - Democratic-Republican

4. JAMES MADISON

Born - 3-16-1751
Died - 6-28-1836
Place of Birth - Port Conway, Virginia
Vice Presidents - George Clinton, Elbridge Gerry
Term in Office - 3-4-1809 to 3-3-1817
Political Party - Democratic-Republican

5. JAMES MONROE

Born - 4-28-1758
Died - 7-4-1831
Place of Birth - Westmoreland Co., Virginia
Vice President - Daniel D. Tompkins
Term in Office - 3-4-1817 to 3-3-1825
Political Party - Democratic-Republican

6. John Quincy Adams

Born - 7-11-1767
Died - 2-23-1848
Place of Birth - Braintree, Massachusetts
Vice President - John C. Calhoun
Term in Office - 3-4-1825 to 3-3-1829
Political Party - Democratic-Republican

7. ANDREW JACKSON

Born - 3-15-1767
Died - 6-8-1845
Place of Birth - Waxhaw, South Carolina
Vice Presidents - John C. Calhoun, Martin Van Buren
Term in Office - 3-4-1829 to 3-3-1837
Political Party - Democratic

8. Martin Van Buren

Born - 12-5-1782
Died - 7-24-1862
Place of Birth - Kinderhook, New York
Vice President - Richard M. Johnson
Term in Office - 3-4-1837 to 3-3-1841
Political Party - Democratic

9. WILLIAM H. HARRISON

Born - 2-9-1773
Died - 4-4-1841
Place of Birth - Berkeley, Virginia
Vice President - John Tyler
Term in Office - 3-4-1841 to 4-4-1841
Political Party - Whig

10. JOHN TYLER

Born - 3-29-1790
Died - 1-18-1862
Place of Birth - Charles City Co., Virginia
Vice President - none
Term in Office - 4-6-1841 to 3-3-1845
Political Party - Whig

11. JAMES K. POLK

Born - 11-2-1795
Died - 6-15-1849
Place of Birth - Mecklenburg Co., North Carolina
Vice President - George M. Dallas
Term in Office - 3-4-1845 to 3-3-1849
Political Party - Democratic

12. ZACHARY TAYLOR

Born - 11-24-1784
Died - 7-9-1850
Place of Birth - Montebello, Virginia
Vice President - Millard Fillmore
Term in Office - 3-4-1849 to 7-9-1850
Political Party - Whig

13. MILLARD FILLMORE

Born - 1-7-1800
Died - 3-8-1874
Place of Birth - Summerhill, New York
Vice President - none
Term in Office - 7-10-1850 to 3-3-1853
Political Party - Whig

14. FRANKLIN PIERCE

Born - 11-23-1804
Died - 10-8-1869
Place of Birth - Hillsborough, New Hampshire
Vice President - William R. King
Term in Office - 3-4-1853 to 3-3-1857
Political Party - Democratic

15. JAMES BUCHANAN

Born - 4-23-1791
Died - 6-1-1868
Place of Birth - Cove Gap, Pennsylvania
Vice President - John C. Breckinridge
Term in Office - 3-4-1857 to 3-3-1861
Political Party - Democratic

16. ABRAHAM LINCOLN

Born - 2-12-1809
Died - 4-15-1865
Place of Birth - Hodgenville, Kentucky
Vice Presidents - Hannibal Hamlin, Andrew Johnson
Term in Office - 3-4-1861 to 4-15-1865
Political Party - Republican

17. ANDREW JOHNSON

Born - 12-29-1808
Died - 7-31-1875
Place of Birth - Raleigh, North Carolina
Vice President - none
Term in Office - 4-15-1865 to 3-3-1869
Political Party - Union

18. Ulysses S. Grant

Born - 4-27-1822
Died - 7-23-1885
Place of Birth - Point Pleasant, Ohio
Vice Presidents - Schuyler Colfax, Henry Wilson
Term in Office - 3-4-1869 to 3-3-1877
Political Party - Republican

19. RUTHERFORD B. HAYES

Born - 10-4-1822
Died - 1-17-1893
Place of Birth - Delaware, Ohio
Vice President - William A. Wheeler
Term in office - 3-4-1877 to 3-3-1881
Political Party - Republican

20. JAMES GARFIELD

Born - 11-19-1831
Died - 9-19-1881
Place of Birth - Orange, Ohio
Vice President - Chester A. Arthur
Term in Office - 3-4-1881 to 9-19-1881
Political Party - Republican

21. Chester A. Arthur

Born - 10-5-1829
Died - 11-18-1886
Place of Birth - Fairfield, Vermont
Vice President - none
Term in Office - 9-20-1881 to 3-3-1885
Political Party - Republican

22. GROVER CLEVELAND

Born - 3-18-1837
Died - 6-24-1908
Place of Birth - Caldwell, New Jersey
Vice President - Thomas A. Hendricks
Term in Office - 3-4-1885 to 3-3-1889
Political Party - Democratic

23. BENJAMIN HARRISON

Born - 8-20-1833
Died - 3-13-1901
Place of Birth - North Bend, Ohio
Vice President - Levi P. Morton
Term in Office - 3-4-1889 to 3-3-1893
Political Party - Republican

24. GROVER CLEVELAND

Born - 3-18-1837
Died - 6-24-1908
Place of Birth - Caldwell, New Jersey
Vice President - Adlai E. Stevenson
Term in Office - 3-4-1893 to 3-3-1897
Political Party - Democratic

25. WILLIAM MCKINLEY

Born - 1-29-1843
Died - 9-14-1901
Place of Birth - Niles, Ohio
Vice Presidents - Garret A. Hobart, Theodore Roosevelt
Term in Office - 3-4-1897 to 9-14-1901
Political Party - Republican

26. THEODORE ROOSEVELT

Born - 10-27-1858
Died - 1-6-1919
Place of Birth - New York, New York
Vice Presidents - None, Charles W. Fairbanks
Term in Office - 9-14-1901 to 3-3-1909
Political Party - Republican

USA FACTBOOK

27. William H. Taft

Born - 9-15-1857
Died - 3-8-1930
Place of Birth - Cincinnati, Ohio
Vice President - James S. Sherman
Term in Office - 3-4-1909 to 3-3-1913
Political Party - Republican

28. WOODROW WILSON

Born - 12-28-1856
Died - 2-3-1924
Place of Birth - Staunton, Virginia
Vice President - Thomas R. Marshall
Term in Office - 3-4-1913 to 3-3-1921
Political Party - Democratic

29. WARREN G. HARDING

Born - 11-2-1865
Died - 8-2-1923
Place of Birth - Corsica, Ohio
Vice President - Calvin Coolidge
Term in Office - 3-4-1921 to 8-2-1923
Political Party - Republican

30. CALVIN COOLIDGE

Born - 7-4-1872
Died - 1-5-1933
Place of Birth - Plymouth, Vermont
Vice Presidents - None, Charles G. Dawes
Term in Office - 8-3-1923 to 3-3-1929
Political Party - Republican

31. HERBERT HOOVER

Born - 8-10-1874
Died - 10-20-1964
Place of Birth - West Branch, Iowa
Vice President - Charles Curtis
Term in Office - 3-4-1929 to 3-3-1933
Political Party - Republican

32. FRANKLIN D. ROOSEVELT

Born - 1-30-1882

Died - 4-12-1945

Place of Birth - Hyde Park, New York

Vice Presidents - John N. Garner, Henry A. Wallace, Harry S. Truman

Term in Office - 3-4-1933 to 4-12-1945

Political Party - Democratic

33. Harry S. Truman

Born - 5-8-1884
Died - 12-26-1972
Place of Birth - Lamar, Missouri
Vice Presidents - None, Alben W. Barkley
Term in Office - 4-12-1945 to 1-20-1953
Political Party - Democratic

34. DWIGHT D. EISENHOWER

Born - 10-14-1890
Died - 3-28-1969
Place of Birth - Denison, Texas
Vice President - Richard M. Nixon
Term in Office - 1-20-1953 to 1-20-1961
Political Party - Republican

35. JOHN F. KENNEDY

Born - 5-29-1917
Died - 11-22-1963
Place of Birth - Brookline, Massachusetts
Vice President - Lyndon B. Johnson
Term in Office - 1-20-1961 to 11-22-1963
Political Party - Democratic

36. Lyndon B. Johnson

Born - 8-27-1908
Died - 1-22-1973
Place of Birth - Near Stonewall, Texas
Vice Presidents - None, Hubert H. Humphrey
Term in Office - 11-22-1963 to 1-20-1969
Political Party - Democratic

37. RICHARD M. NIXON

Born - 1-9-1913
Died - 4-22-1994
Place of Birth - Yorba Linda, California
Vice Presidents - Spiro T. Agnew, Gerald R. Ford
Term in Office - 1-20-1969 to 8-9-1974
Political Party - Republican

38. GERALD R. FORD

Born - 7-14-1913
Died - _____
Place of Birth - Omaha, Nebraska
Vice President - Nelson A. Rockefeller
Term in Office - 9-9-1974 to 1-20-1977
Political Party - Republican

39. JAMES CARTER

Born - 10-1-1924
Died - _____
Place of Birth - Plains, Georgia
Vice President - Walter F. Mondale
Term in Office - 1-20-1977 to 1-20-1981
Political Party - Democratic

40. RONALD REAGAN

Born - 2-6-1911
Died - 6-5-2004
Place of Birth - Tampico, Illinois
Vice President - George H.W. Bush
Term in Office - 1-20-1981 to 1-20-1989
Political Party - Republican

41. GEORGE H.W. BUSH

Born - 6-12-1924
Died - _____
Place of Birth - Milton, Massachusetts
Vice President - J. Danforth Quayle
Term in Office - 1-20-1989 to 1-20-1993
Political Party - Republican

42. William Clinton

Born - 8-19-1946
Died - _____
Place of Birth - Hope, Arkansas
Vice President - Albert Gore, Jr.
Term in Office - 1-20-1993 to 1-20-2001
Political Party - Democratic

43. GEORGE W. BUSH

Born - 7-6-1946
Died - _____
Place of Birth - New Haven, Connecticut
Vice President - Richard B. Cheney
Term in Office - 1-20-2001 to _____
Political Party - Republican

44.

Born -
Died -
Place of Birth -
Vice President -
Term in Office -
Political Party -

45.

Born -
Died -
Place of Birth -
Vice President -
Term in Office -
Political Party -

46.

Born -
Died -
Place of Birth -
Vice President -
Term in Office -
Political Party -

THE DECLARATION
OF INDEPENDENCE

THE DECLARATION OF INDEPENDENCE WAS ADOPTED JULY 4, 1776 AND WRITTEN BY THOMAS JEFFERSON.

PREAMBLE:

When in the Course of human events, it becomes necessary for one people to dissolve the political bands which have connected them with another, and to assume among the powers of the earth, the separate and equal station to which the Laws of Nature and of Nature's God entitle them, a decent respect to the opinions of mankind requires that they should declare the causes which impel them to the separation.

THE RIGHT OF THE PEOPLE TO CONTROL THEIR GOVERNMENT:

We hold these truths to be self-evident, that all men are created equal, that they are endowed by their Creator with certain unalienable Rights, that among these are Life, Liberty and the pursuit of Happiness; that to secure these rights, Governments are instituted among Men, deriving their just powers from the consent of the governed, – That whenever any Form of Government becomes destructive of these ends, it is the Right of the People to alter or to abolish it, and to institute new Government, laying its foundation on such principles and organizing its powers in such form, as to them shall

seem most likely to effect their Safety and Happiness. Prudence, indeed, will dictate that Governments long established should not be changed for light and transient causes; and accordingly all experience hath shewn that mankind are more disposed to suffer, while evils are sufferable, than to right themselves by abolishing the forms to which they are accustomed. But when a long train of abuses and usurpations, pursuing invariably the same Object evinces a design to reduce them under absolute Despotism, it is their right, it is their duty, to throw off such Government, and to provide new Guards for their future security. – Such has been the patient sufferance of these Colonies; and such is now the necessity which constrains them to alter their former Systems of Government. The history of the present King of Great Britain is a history of repeated injuries and usurpations, all having in direct object the establishment of an absolute Tyranny over these States. To prove this, let facts be submitted to a candid world.

TYRANNICAL ACTS OF THE BRITISH KING:

He has refused his Assent to Laws, the most wholesome and necessary for the public good.

He has forbidden his Governors to pass Laws of immediate and pressing importance, unless suspended in their operation till his Assent should be obtained; and when so suspended, he has utterly neglected to attend to them.

He has refused to pass other Laws for the accommodation of large districts of people, unless those people would relinquish the right of Representation in the Legislature, a right inestimable to them and formidable to tyrants only.

He has called together legislative bodies at places unusual, uncomfortable, and distant from the depository of their Public Records, for the sole purpose of fatiguing them into compliance with his measures.

He has dissolved Representative Houses repeatedly, for opposing with manly firmness his invasions on the rights of the people.

He has refused for a long time, after such dissolutions, to cause others to be elected, whereby the Legislative Powers, incapable of Annihilation, have returned to the People at large for their exercise; the State remaining in the mean time exposed to all the dangers of invasion from without, and convulsions within.

He has endeavored to prevent the population of these States; for that purpose obstructing the Laws for Naturalization of Foreigners; refusing to pass others to encourage their migrations hither, and raising the conditions of new Appropriations of Lands.

He has obstructed the Administration of Justice, by refusing his Assent to Laws for establishing Judiciary Powers.

He has made Judges dependent on his Will alone, for the tenure of their offices, and the amount and payment of their salaries.

He has erected a multitude of New Offices, and sent hither swarms of Officers to harass our people and eat out their substance.

He has kept among us, in times of peace, Standing Armies without the Consent of our legislatures.

He has affected to render the Military independent of and superior to the Civil Power. He has combined with others to subject us to a jurisdiction foreign to our constitution, and unacknowledged by our laws; giving his Assent to their Acts of pretended Legislation:

For quartering large bodies of armed troops among us:

For protecting them, by a mock Trial, from punishment for any Murders which they should commit on the Inhabitants of these States:

For cutting off our Trade with all parts of the world:

For imposing Taxes on us without our Consent:

For depriving us in many cases, of the benefit of Trial by Jury:

For transporting us beyond Seas to be tried for pretended offences:

For abolishing the free System of English Laws in a neighboring Province, establishing therein an Arbitrary government, and enlarging its Boundaries so as to render it at once an example and fit instrument for introducing the same absolute rule into these Colonies

For taking away our Charters, abolishing our most valuable Laws and altering fundamentally the Forms of

our Governments:

For suspending our own Legislatures, and declaring themselves invested with power to legislate for us in all cases whatsoever.

He has abdicated Government here, by declaring us out of his Protection and waging War against us.

He has plundered our seas, ravaged our Coasts, burnt our towns, and destroyed the lives of our people.

He is at this time transporting large Armies of foreign Mercenaries to complete the works of death, desolation, and tyranny, already begun with circumstances of Cruelty & Perfidy scarcely paralleled in the most barbarous ages, and totally unworthy the Head of a civilized nation.

He has constrained our fellow Citizens taken Captive on the high Seas to bear Arms against their Country, to become the executioners of their friends and Brethren, or to fall themselves by their Hands.

He has excited domestic insurrections amongst us, and has endeavored to bring on the inhabitants of our frontiers the merciless Indian Savages, whose known rule of warfare is an undistinguished destruction of all ages, sexes and conditions.

EFFORTS OF THE COLONIES TO AVOID SEPARATION:

In every stage of these Oppressions We have Petitioned for Redress in the most humble terms: Our repeated Petitions have been answered only by repeated injury. A Prince, whose character is thus marked by every act which may define a Tyrant, is unfit to be the ruler of a free people.

Nor have We been wanting in attentions to our British brethren. We have warned them from time to time of attempts by their legislature to extend an unwarrantable jurisdiction over us. We have reminded them of the circumstances of our emigration and settlement here. We have appealed to their native justice and magnanimity, and we have conjured them by the ties of our common kindred to disavow these usurpations, which would inevitably interrupt our connections and correspondence. They too have been deaf to the voice of justice and of consanguinity. We must, therefore, acquiesce in the necessity, which denounces our Separation, and hold them, as we hold the rest of mankind, Enemies in War, in Peace Friends.

THE COLONIES ARE DECLARED FREE AND INDEPENDENT:

We, therefore, the Representatives of the United States of America, in General Congress, Assembled, appealing to the Supreme Judge of the world for the rectitude of our intentions, do, in the Name, and by Authority of

the good People of these Colonies, solemnly publish and declare, That these United Colonies are, and of Right ought to be Free and Independent States; that they are Absolved from all Allegiance to the British Crown, and that all political connection between them and the State of Great Britain, is and ought to be totally dissolved; and that as Free and Independent States, they have full Power to levy War, conclude Peace contract Alliances, establish Commerce, and to do all other Acts and Things which Independent States may of right do.

And for the support of this Declaration, with a firm reliance on the protection of Divine Providence, we mutually pledge to each other our Lives, our Fortunes and our sacred Honor.

Signed by:

John Hancock: President, from Massachusetts

Georgia – Button Gwinnett; Lyman Hall; George Walton

Rhone Island – Stephen Hopkins; William Ellery

Connecticut – Roger Sherman; Samuel Huntington; William Williams; Oliver Wolcott

North Carolina – William Hooper; Joseph Hewes; John Penn

South Carolina – Edward Rutledge; Thomas Heyward, Jr.; Thomas Lynch, Jr.; Arthur Middleton

Maryland – Samuel Chase; William Paca; Thomas Stone; Charles Carroll

Virginia – George Wythe, Richard Henry Lee; Thomas Jefferson; Benjamin Harrison; Thomas Nelson, Jr.; Francis Lightfoot Lee; Carter Braxton

Pennsylvania – Robert Morris; Benjamin Rush; Benjamin Franklin; John Morton; George Clymer; James Smith; George Taylor; James Wilson, George Ross

Delaware – Caesar Rodney; George Read; Thomas McKean

New York – William Floyd; Philip Livingston; Francis Lewis; Lewis Morris

New Jersey – Richard Stockton; John Witherspoon; Francis Hopkinson; John Hart; Abraham Clark

New Hampshire – Josiah Barlett; William Whipple; Matthew Thornton

Massachusetts – Samuel Adams, John Adams, Robert Treat Paine; Elbridge Gerry

THE CONSTITUTION OF THE UNITED STATES OF AMERICA

(Items in italics were altered by various amendments)

PREAMBLE – PURPOSE OF THE CONSTITUTION

We the people of the United States, in order to form a more perfect Union, establish justice, insure domestic tranquility, provide for the common defense, promote the general welfare, and secure the blessings of liberty to ourselves and our posterity, do ordain and establish the Constitution for the United States of America.

ARTICLE 1. THE LEGISLATURE

Section 1. Congress

All legislative powers herein granted shall be vested in a Congress of the United States, which shall consist of a Senate and a House of Representatives.

Section 2. The House of Representatives

1. Elections – The House of Representatives shall be composed of members chosen every second year by the people of the several states, and the electors in each state shall have the qualifications requisite for electors of the most numerous branch of the state legislature.

2. Qualifications – No Person shall be a Representative who shall not have attained to the age of twenty five years, and been seven years a citizen of the United States, and who shall not, when elected, be an inhabitant of that state in which he shall be chosen.

3. Number of Representatives – Representatives *and direct taxes* shall be apportioned among the several states which may be included within this Union,

USA FACTBOOK

according to their respective numbers, *which shall be determined by adding to the whole number of free persons, including those bound to service for a term of years, and excluding Indians not taxed, 3/5 of all other persons.* The actual enumeration shall be made within 3 years after the first meeting of the Congress of the United States, and within every subsequent term of 10 years, in such manner as they shall by law direct. The number of Representatives shall not exceed 1 for every 30,000 but each state shall have at least 1 Representative; *and until such enumeration shall be made, the state of New Hampshire shall be entitled to choose 3, Massachusetts 8, Rhone Island and Providence Plantations 1, Connecticut 5, New York 6, New Jersey 4, Pennsylvania 8, Delaware 1, Maryland 6, Virginia 10, North Carolina 5, South Carolina 5, and Georgia 3.*

4. Vacancies – When vacancies happen in the representation from any state, the executive authority thereof shall issue writs of election to fill such vacancies.

5. Officers and Impeachment – The House of Representatives shall choose their Speaker and other officers; and shall have the sole power of impeachment.

Section 3. The Senate

1. Numbers – The Senate of the United States shall be composed of 2 Senators from each state, *chosen by the legislature thereof,* for 6 years; and each Senator shall have 1 vote.

2. Classifying Terms – Immediately after they shall be

assembled in consequence of the first election, they shall be divided as equally as may be into 3 classes. The seats of the Senators of the first class shall be vacated at the expiration of the second year, of the second class at the expiration of the fourth year, and of the third class at the expiration of the sixth year, so that 1/3 may be chosen every second year; *and if vacancies happen by resignation, or otherwise, during the recess of the legislature of any state, the executive thereof may make temporary appointments until the next meeting of the legislature, which shall then fill such vacancies.*

3. Qualifications – No person shall be a Senator who shall not have attained to the age of 30 years, and been 9 years a citizen of the United States, and who shall not, when elected, be an inhabitant of that state for which he shall be chosen.

4. Role of Vice-President – The Vice-President of the United States shall be President of the Senate, but shall have no vote, unless they be equally divided.

5. Officers – The Senate shall choose their other officers, and also a President pro tempore, in the absence of the Vice-President, or when he shall exercise the office of the President of the United States.

6. Impeachment Trials – The Senate shall have the sole power to try all impeachments. When sitting for that purpose, they shall be on oath or affirmation. When the President of the United States is tried, the Chief Justice shall preside: and no person shall be convicted without the concurrence of 2/3 of the members present.

7. Punishment for Impeachment – Judgement in the

cases of impeachment shall not extend further than to removal from office, and disqualification to hold and enjoy any office of honor, trust or profit under the United States; but the party convicted shall never the less be liable and subject to indictment, trial, judgement and punishment, according to law.

Section 4. Congressional Elections

1. Regulations – The times, places and manner of holding elections for Senators and Representatives shall be prescribed in each state by the legislature thereof; but the Congress may at any time by law make or alter such regulations, except as to the places of choosing Senators.

2. Sessions – The Congress shall assemble at least once every year, *and such meeting shall be on the first Monday in December, unless they shall by law appoint a different day.*

Section 5. Rules and Procedures

1. Quorum – Each house shall be the judge of the elections, returns, and qualifications of its own members, and a majority of each shall constitute a quorum to do business; but a smaller number may adjourn from day to day, and may be authorized to compel the attendance of absent members, in such manner, and under such penalties as each house may provide.

2. Rules and Conduct – Each house may determine the rules of its proceedings, punish its members for disorderly behavior, and, with the concurrence of 2/3, expel a member.

3. Congressional Records – Each house shall keep a journal of its proceedings, and from time to time publish the same, excepting such parts as may in their judgements require secrecy; and the yeas and nays of the members of either house on any question shall, at the desire of 1/5 of those present, be entered on the journal.

4. Adjournment – Neither house, during the session of the Congress, shall, without the consent of the other, adjourn for more than 3 days, nor to any other place than that in which the 2 houses shall be sitting.

Section 6. Payment and Privileges

1. Salary – The Senators and the Representatives shall receive a compensation for their services, to be ascertained by law, and paid out of the treasury of the United States. They shall in all cases, except treason, felony and breach of the peace, be privileged from arrest during their attendance at the session of their respective houses, and in going to and returning from the same; and for any speech or debate in either house, they shall not be questioned in any other place.

2. Restrictions – No Senator or Representative shall, during the time for which he was elected, be appointed to any civil office under the authority of the United States, which shall have been created, or the emoluments whereof shall have been increased during such time; and no person holding any office under the United States, shall be a member of either house during his continuance in office.

Section 7. How a Bill Becomes a Law

1. Tax Bills – All bills for raising revenue shall originate in the House of Representatives; but the Senate may propose or concur with amendments as on other Bills.

2. Lawmaking Process – Every bill which shall have passed the House of Representatives and the Senate, shall, before it becomes a law, be presented to the President of the United States: if he approves he shall sign it, but if not he shall return it, with his objections to that house in which it shall have originated, who shall enter the objections at large on their journal, and proceed to reconsider it. If after such reconsideration 2/3 of that house shall agree to pass the bill, it shall be sent, together with the objections, to the other house, by which it shall likewise be reconsidered, and if approved by 2/3 of that house, it shall become a law. But in all such cases the votes of both houses shall be determined by yeas and nays, and the names of the persons voting for and against the bill shall be entered on the journal of each house respectively. If any bill shall not be returned by the President within 10 days (Sundays excepted) after it shall have been presented to him, the same shall be a law, in like manner as if he had signed it, unless the Congress by their adjournment prevent its return, in which case it shall not be a law.

3. Role of the President – Every order, resolution, or vote to which the concurrence of the Senate and the House of Representatives may be necessary (except on a question of adjournment) shall be presented to the President of the United States; and before the same

shall take effect, shall be approved by him, or being disapproved by him, shall be repassed by 2/3 of the Senate and the House of Representatives, according to the rules and limitations prescribed in the case of a bill.

Section 8. Powers granted to Congress

1. Taxation – The Congress shall have power to lay and collect taxes, duties, imposts and excises, to pay the debts and provide for the common defense and general welfare of the Unites States; but all duties, imposts and excises shall be uniform throughout the United States;

2. Credit – To borrow money on the credit of the United States;

3. Commerce – To regulate commerce with foreign nations, and among the several states, and with the Indian Tribes;

4. Naturalization, Bankruptcy – To establish a uniform rule of naturalization, and uniform laws on the subject of bankruptcies throughout the United States;

5. Money – To coin money, regulate the value thereof, and of foreign coin, and fix the standard of weights and measures;

6. Counterfeiting – To provide for the punishment of counterfeiting the securities and current coin of the United States;

7. Post Office – To establish post offices and post roads;

8. Patents, Copyrights – To promote the progress of science and useful arts, by securing for limited times to authors and inventors the exclusive right to their

respective writings and discoveries;

9. Federal Courts – To constitute tribunals inferior to the Supreme Court;

10. International Law – To define and punish piracies and felonies committed on high seas, and offenses against the law of nations;

11. War – To declare war, grant letters of marque and reprisal, and make rules concerning captures on land and water;

12. Army – To raise and support armies, but no appropriation of money to that use shall be for a longer term than 2 years;

13. Navy – To provide and maintain a navy;

14. Regulation of Armed Forces – To make rules for the government and regulation of the land and naval forces;

15. Militia – To provide for calling forth the militia to execute the laws of the Union, suppress insurrections and repel invasions;

16. Regulations for Militia – To provide for organizing, arming, and disciplining the militia, and for governing such part of them as may be employed in the service of the United States, reserving to the states respectively the appointment of the officers, and the authority of training the militia according to the discipline prescribed by Congress;

17. District of Columbia – To exercise exclusive legislation in all cases whatsoever, over such district (not

exceeding 10 miles square) as may, by cession of particular states, and the acceptance of Congress, become the seat of the government of the United States, and to exercise like authority over all places purchased by the consent of the legislature of the state in which the same shall be, for the erection of forts, magazines, arsenals, dockyards, and other needful buildings; – and

18. Elastic Clause – To make all laws which shall be necessary and proper for carrying into execution the foregoing powers, and all the other powers vested by this Constitution in the government of the United States, or in any department or officer thereof.

Section 9. Powers Denied Congress

1. *Slave trade – The migration or importation of such persons as any of the states now existing shall think proper to admit, shall not be prohibited by the Congress prior to the year 1808, but a tax or duty may be imposed on such importation, not exceeding $10 for each person.*

2. Habeas Corpus – The privilege of the writ of habeas corpus shall not be suspended, unless when in cases of rebellion or invasion the public safety may require it.

3. Illegal Punishment – No bill of attainder or ex post facto law shall be passed.

4. Direct Taxes – No capitation, *or other direct*, tax shall be laid, *unless in proportion to the census or enumeration herein before directed to be taken.*

5. Export Taxes – No tax or duty shall be laid on articles exported from any state.

6. No Favorites – No preference shall be given by any regulation of commerce or revenue to the ports of one state over those of another: nor shall vessels bound to, or from, one state be obliged to enter, clear, or pay duties in another.

7. Public Money – No money shall be drawn from the treasury, but in consequence of appropriations made by law; and a regular statement and account of the receipts and expenditures of all public money shall be published from time to time.

8. Titles of Nobility – No title of nobility shall be granted by the United States: and no person holding any office of profit or trust under them shall, without the consent of the Congress, accept of any present, emolument, office, or title, of any kind whatever, from any King, prince, or foreign state.

Section 10. Powers Denied the States

1. Restrictions – No state shall enter into any treaty, alliance, or confederation; grant letters of marque and reprisal; coin money; emit bills of credit; make anything but gold and silver coin a tender in payment of debts; pass any bill of attainder, ex post facto law, or law impairing the obligation of contracts, or grant any title of nobility.

2. Import and Export Taxes – No state shall, without the consent of Congress, lay any imposts or duties on imports or exports, except what may be absolutely necessary for executing its inspection laws; and the net produce of all duties and imposts, laid by any state on imports or exports, shall be for the use of the treasury

of the United States; and all such laws shall be subject to the revision and control of the Congress.

3. Peacetime and War Restraints – No state shall, without the consent of Congress, lay any duty of tonnage, keep troops or ships of war in any time of peace, enter into any agreement or compact with another state, or with a foreign power, or engage in war, unless actually invaded, or in such imminent danger as will not admit of delay.

ARTICLE 2. THE EXECUTIVE

Section 1. The Presidency

1. Terms of Office – The executive power shall be vested in a President of the United States of America. He shall hold his office during the term of 4 years, and, together with the Vice- President, chosen for the same term, be elected, as follows:

2. Electoral College – Each state shall appoint, in such manner as the Legislature thereof may direct, a number of electors, equal to the whole number of Senators and Representatives to which the State may be entitled in the Congress; but no Senator or Representative, or person holding an office of trust or profit under the United States, shall be appointed an elector.

3. *Former Method of Electing President – The Electors shall meet in their respective states, and vote by ballot for 2 persons, of whom 1 at least shall not be an inhabitant of the same state with themselves. And they shall*

make a list of all persons voted for, and of the number of votes for each; which list they shall sign and certify, and transmit sealed to the seat of the government of the United States, directed to the President of the Senate. The President of the Senate shall, in the presence of the Senate and the House of Representatives, open all the certificates, and the votes shall then be counted. The person having the greatest number of votes shall be the President, if such number be a majority of the whole number of electors appointed; and if there be more than one who have such majority, and have an equal number of votes, then the House of Representatives shall immediately choose by ballot one of them for President; and if no person have a majority, then from the 5 highest on the list the said House shall in like manner choose the President. But in choosing the President, the votes shall be taken by States, the representation from each state having one vote; a quorum for this purpose shall consist of a member or members from 2/3 of the states, and a majority of all the states shall be necessary to a choice. In every case, after the choice of the President, the person having the greatest number of votes of the electors shall be the Vice-President. But if there should remain 2 or more who have equal votes, the Senate shall choose from them by ballot the Vice-President.

4. Election Day – The Congress may determine the time of choosing the electors, and the day on which they shall give their votes, which day shall be the same throughout the United States.

5. Qualifications – No person except a natural-born

USA FACTBOOK

citizen, *or a citizen of the United States at the time of the adoption of this Constitution*, shall be eligible to the office of President; neither shall any person be eligible to that office who shall not have attained to the age of 35 years, and been 14 years a resident within the United States.

6. Succession – In case of the removal of the President from office, or of his death, resignation, or inability to discharge the powers and the duties of the said office, the same shall devolve on the Vice-President, and the Congress may by law provide for the case of removal, death, resignation or inability, both of the President and Vice-President, declaring what officer shall then act as President, and such officer shall act accordingly, until the disability be removed, or a President shall be elected.

7. Salary – The President shall, at stated times, receive for his services, a compensation, which shall neither be increased nor diminished during the period for which he shall have been elected, and he shall not receive within that period any other emolument from the United States, or any of them.

8. Oath of Office – Before he enter on the execution of his office, he shall take the following oath or affirmation: – "I do solemnly swear (or affirm) that I will faithfully execute the office of the President of the United States, and will to the best of my ability, preserve, protect and defend the Constitution of the United States."

Section 2. Powers of the President

1. Military Powers – The President shall be

commander in chief of the Army and Navy of the United States, and of the militia of the several states, when called into the actual service of the United States; he may require the opinion, in writing, of the principal officer in each of the executive departments, upon any subject relating to the duties of their respective offices, and he shall have power to grant reprieves and pardons for offenses against the United States, except in cases of impeachment.

2. Treaties, Appointments – He shall have power, by and with the advise and consent of the Senate, to make treaties, provided 2/3 of the Senators present concur; and he shall nominate, and by and with the advice and consent of the Senate, shall appoint ambassadors, other public ministers and consuls, judges of the Supreme Court, and all other officers of the United States, whose appointments are not herein otherwise provided for, and which shall be established by law; but the Congress may by law vest the appointment of such inferior officers, as they think proper, in the President alone, in the courts of law, or in the heads of departments.

3. Vacancies – The President shall have power to fill up all vacancies that may happen during the recess of the Senate, by granting commissions which shall expire at the end of their next session.

Section 3. Presidential Duties

He shall from time to time give to the Congress information of the State of the Union, and recommend to their consideration such measures as he shall judge necessary and expedient; he may, on extraordinary

occasions, convene both houses, or either of them, and in case of disagreement between them, with respect to the time of adjournment, he may adjourn them to such time as he shall think proper; he shall receive ambassadors and other public ministers; he shall take care that the laws be faithfully executed, and shall commission all the officers of the United States.

Section 4. Impeachment

The President, Vice-President and all civil officers of the United States shall be removed from office on Impeachment for, and conviction of, treason, bribery, or other high crimes and misdemeanors.

ARTICLE 3. THE JUDICIARY

Section 1. Federal Courts and Judges

The judicial power of the United States shall be vested in one Supreme Court, and in such inferior courts as the Congress may from time to time ordain and establish. The judges, both of the Supreme and inferior courts, shall hold their offices during good behavior, and shall, at stated times, receive for their services a compensation, which shall not be diminished during their continuance in office.

Section 2. The Courts' Authority

1. General Authority – The judicial power shall extend to all cases, in law and equity, arising under this Constitution, the laws of the United States, and treaties made, or which shall be made, under their authority; –

to all cases affecting ambassadors, other public ministers and consuls; – to all cases of admiralty and maritime jurisdiction; – to controversies to which the United States shall be a party; – to controversies between 2 or more states; – *between a state and citizens of another state*; – between citizens of different states; – between citizens of the same state claming lands under grants of different states, *and between a state, or the citizens thereof, and foreign states, citizens or subjects.*

2. Supreme Court – In all cases affecting ambassadors, other public ministers and consuls, and those in which a state shall be party, the Supreme Court shall have original jurisdiction. In all the other cases before mentioned, the Supreme Court shall have appellate jurisdiction, both as to law and fact, with such exceptions, and under such regulations, as the Congress shall make.

3. Trial by Jury – The trial of all crimes, except in cases of impeachment, shall be by jury; and such trial shall be held in the state where the said crimes shall have-been committed; but when not committed within any state, the trial shall be at such place or places as the Congress may by law have directed.

Section 3. Treason

1. Definition – Treason against the United States shall consist only in levying war against them, or in adhering to there enemies, giving them aid and comfort. No person shall be convicted of treason unless on the testimony of 2 witnesses to the same overt act, or on confession in open court.

2. Punishment – The Congress shall have power to declare the punishment of treason, but no attainder of treason shall work corruption of blood, or forfeiture except during the life of the person attained.

ARTICLE 4. RELATIONS AMONG STATES

Section 1. State Acts and Records

Full Faith and credit shall be given in each state to the public acts, records, and judicial proceedings of every other state. And the Congress may by general laws prescribe the manner in which such acts, records and proceedings shall be proved, and the affect thereof.

Section 2. Rights of Citizens

1. Citizenship – The citizens of each state shall be entitled to all privileges and immunities of citizens in the several states.

2. Extradition – A person charged in any state with treason, felony, or other crime, who shall flee from justice, and be found in another state, shall on demand of the executive authority of the state from which he fled, be delivered up, to be removed to the state having jurisdiction of the crime.

3. *Fugitive Slaves – No person held to service or labor in one state, under the laws thereof, escaping into another, shall, in consequence of any law or regulation therein, be discharged from such service or labor, but shall be delivered up on claim of the party to whom such service or labor may be due.*

Section 3. New States

1. Admission – New states may be admitted by the Congress into this Union; but no new state shall be formed or erected within the jurisdiction of any other state; nor any state be formed by the junction of 2 or more states, or parts of states, without the consent of the legislatures of the states concerned as well as of the Congress.

2. Congressional Authority – The Congress shall have power to dispose of and make all needful rules and regulations respecting the territory or other property belonging to the United States; and nothing in this Constitution shall be so construed as to prejudice any claims of the United States, or of any particular state.

ARTICLE 5. AMENDING THE CONSTITUTION

The Congress, whenever 2/3 of both houses shall deem it necessary, shall propose amendments to this Constitution, or, on the application of the legislatures of 2/3 of the several states, shall call a convention for proposing amendments, which, in either case, shall be valid to all intents and purposes, as part of this Constitution, when ratified by the legislatures of ¾ of the several states, or by conventions in ¾ thereof, as the one or the other mode of ratification may be proposed by the Congress; *provided that no amendment which may be made prior to the year1808 shall in any manner affect the first and forth clauses in the ninth section of the first article*; and that no state, without its consent,

shall be deprived of its equal suffrage in the Senate.

ARTICLE 6. SUPREMACY OF THE NATIONAL GOVERNMENT

Section 1. Valid Debts

All debts contracted and engagements entered into, before the adoption of this Constitution, shall be as valid against the United States under this constitution, as under the Confederation.

Section 2. Supreme Law

This Constitution, and the laws of the United States which shall be made in pursuance thereof; and all treaties made, or which shall be made, under the authority of the United States, shall be the supreme law of the land; and the judges in every state shall be bound thereby, anything in the Constitution or laws of any state to the contrary notwithstanding.

Section 3. Loyalty to the Constitution

The Senators and Representatives before mentioned, and the members of the several state legislatures, and all executive and judicial officers, both of the United States and of the several states, shall be bound by oath or affirmation to support this Constitution; but no religious test shall ever be required as a qualification to any office or public trust under the United States.

ARTICLE 7. RATIFICATION

The ratification of the conventions of 9 states shall be sufficient for the establishment of this Constitution between the states so ratifying the same. Done in the convention by the unanimous consent of the states present, the 17th day of September in the year of our Lord 1787 and of the independence of the United States of America the 12th. In witness whereof we have here unto subscribed our names.

George Washington: President and deputy from Virginia

New Hampshire: John Langdon, Nicholas Gilman

Massachusetts: Nathaniel Gorham, Rufus King

Connecticut: William Samuel Johnson, Roger Sherman

New York: Alexander Hamilton

New Jersey: William Livingston, David Brearley, William Paterson, Jonathan Dayton

Pennsylvania: Benjamin Franklin, Thomas Mifflin, Robert Morris, George Clymer, Thomas FitzSimons, Jared Ingersoll, James Wilson, Gouverneur Morris

Delaware: George Read, Gunning Bedford Jr., John Dickinson, Richard Bassett, Jacob Broom

Maryland: James McHenry, Dan of St. Thomas Jenifer, Daniel Carroll

Virginia: John Blair, James Madison Jr.

North Carolina: William Blount, Richard Dobbs Spaight, Hugh Williamson

South Carolina: John Rutledge, Charles Cotesworth Pinckney, Charles Pinckney, Pierce Butler

Georgia: William Few, Abraham Baldwin

THE BILL OF RIGHTS
AND AMENDMENTS 11-27

Amendments 1-10. The Bill of Rights

Amendment 1. Religious and Political Freedom (1791)

Congress shall make no law respecting an establishment of religion, or prohibiting the free exercise thereof; or abridging the freedom of speech, or of the press; or the right of the people peaceably to assemble, and to petition the Government for a redress of grievances.

Amendment 2. Right to Bear Arms (1791)

A well-regulated militia, being necessary to the security of a free state, the right of the people to keep and bear arms, shall not be infringed.

Amendment 3. Quartering Troops (1791)

No soldier shall, in time of peace be quartered in any house, without the consent of the owner, nor in time of war, but in a manner to be prescribed by law.

Amendment 4. Search and Seizure (1791)

The right of the people to be secure in their persons, houses, papers, and effects, against unreasonable searches and seizures, shall not be violated, and no warrants shall issue, but upon probable cause, supported by oath or affirmation, and particularly describing the place to be searched, and the persons or things to be seized.

Amendment 5. Rights of Accused Person (1791)

No person shall be held to answer for a capital, or otherwise infamous crime, unless on a presentment or

indictment of a Grand Jury, except in cases arising in the land or naval forces, or in the militia, when in actual service in time of war or public danger; nor shall any person be subject for the same offence to be twice put in jeopardy of life or limb; nor shall be compelled in any criminal case to be a witness against himself, nor be deprived of life, liberty, or property, without due process of law; nor shall private property be taken for public use, without just compensation.

Amendment 6. Right to a Speedy, Public Trial (1791)

In all criminal prosecutions, the accused shall enjoy the right to a speedy and public trial, by an impartial jury of the State and district wherein the crime shall have been committed, which district shall have been previously ascertained by law, and to be informed of the nature and cause of the accusation; to be confronted with the witness against him; to have compulsory process for obtaining witnesses in his favor, and to have the assistance of counsel for his defense.

Amendment 7. Trial by Jury in Civil Cases (1791)

In suits at common law, where the value in controversy shall exceed $20, the right of a trial by jury shall be preserved, and no fact tried by a jury, shall be otherwise reexamined in any court of the United States, than according to the rules of the common law.

Amendment 8. Limits of Fines and Punishments (1791)

Excessive bail shall not be required, nor excessive fines

USA FACTBOOK

imposed, nor cruel and unusual punishments inflicted.

Amendment 9. Rights of People (1791)

The enumeration in the Constitution of certain rights shall not be construed to deny or disparage others retained by the people.

Amendment 10. Powers of States and People (1791)

The powers not delegated to the United States by the Constitution, nor prohibited by it to the States, are reserved to the States respectively, or to the people.

AMENDMENTS 11 – 27

Amendment 11. Lawsuits Against States (1798)

Passed by Congress March 4, 1794.

Ratified February 7, 1795. Proclaimed 1798.

Note: Article 3, Section 2, of the Constitution was modified by Amendment 11.

The Judicial power of the United States shall not be construed to extend to any suit in law or equity, commenced or prosecuted against one of the United States by citizens of another state, or by citizens or subjects of a foreign state.

Amendment 12. Election of Executives (1804)

Passed by Congress December 9, 1803.

Ratified June 15, 1804.

Note: Part of Article 2, Section 1, of the Constitution was replaced by Amendment 12.

The electors shall meet in their respective states and vote by ballot for President and Vice-President, one of whom, at least, shall not be an inhabitant of the same state with themselves; they shall name in their ballots the person voted for as President, and in distinct ballots the person voted for as Vice-President, and they shall make distinct lists of all persons voted for as President, and of all persons voted for as Vice-President, and of the number of votes for each, which list they shall sign and certify, and transmit sealed to the seat of the government of the United States, directed to the President of the Senate; - The President of the Senate shall, in the presence of the Senate and House of Representatives, open all the certificates and the votes shall then be counted; - the person having the greatest number of votes for President, shall be the President, if such number be a majority of the whole number of electors appointed; and if no person have such majority, then from the persons having the highest number not exceeding three on the list of those voted for as President, the House of Representatives shall choose immediately, by ballot, the President. But in choosing the President, the votes shall be taken by states, the representation from each state having one vote; a quorum for this purpose shall consist of a member or members from 2/3 of the states, and a majority of the states shall be necessary to a choice. And if the House of Representatives shall not choose a President whenever the right of choice shall devolve upon them, *before the fourth day of March next following*, then the

Vice-President shall act as President, as in the case of death or other constitutional disability of the President. The person having the greatest number of votes as Vice-President, shall be the Vice-President, if such a number be a majority of the whole number of Electors appointed, and if no person have a majority, then from the two highest numbers on the list, the Senate shall choose the Vice-President; a quorum for this purpose shall consist of 2/3 of the whole number of Senators, and a majority of the whole number shall be necessary to a choice. But no person constitutionally ineligible to the office of President shall be eligible to that of Vice-President of the United States.

Amendment 13. Slavery Abolished (1865)

Passed by Congress January 31, 1865.

Ratified December 6, 1865.

Note: A portion of Article 4, Section 2, of the Constitution was superseded by Amendment 13.

Section 1.

Neither slavery or involuntary servitude, except as a punishment for crime whereof the party shall have been duly convicted, shall exist within the United States, or any place subject to their jurisdiction.

Section 2.

Congress shall have power to enforce this article by appropriate legislation.

Amendment 14. Civil Rights (1868)

Passed by Congress June 13, 1866.

Ratified July 9, 1868.

Note: Article 1, Section 2, of the Constitution was modified by Section 2 of Amendment 14.

Section 1.

All persons born or naturalized in the United States, and subject to the jurisdiction thereof, are citizens of the United States and of the state wherein they reside. No state shall make or enforce any law which shall abridge the privileges or immunities of citizens of the United States; nor shall any state deprive any person of life, liberty, or property, without due process of law; nor deny to any person within its jurisdiction the equal protection of the laws.

Section 2.

Representatives shall be apportioned among the several states according to their respective numbers, counting the whole number of persons in each state, excluding Indians not taxed. But when the right to vote at any election for the choice of electors for President and Vice-President of the United States, Representatives in Congress, the executive and judicial officers of a state, or the members of the legislature thereof, is denied to any of the male inhabitants of such state, being 21 years of age, and citizens of the United States, or in any way abridged, except for participation in rebellion, or other crime, the basis of representation therein shall be reduced in the proportion which the number of such

male citizens shall bear to the whole number of male citizens 21 years of age in such state.

Section 3.

No person shall be a Senator or Representative in Congress, or elector of President and Vice-President, or hold any office, civil or military, under the United States, or under any state, who, having previously taken an oath, as a member of Congress, or as an officer of the United States, or as a member of any state legislature, or as an executive or judicial officer of any state, to support the Constitution of the United States, shall have engaged in insurrection or rebellion against the same, or given aid or comfort to the enemies thereof. But Congress may, by a vote of 2/3 of each house, remove such disability.

Section 4.

The validity of the public debt of the United States, authorized by law, including debts incurred for payment of pensions and bounties for services in suppressing insurrection or rebellion, shall not be questioned. But neither the United States nor any state shall assume or pay any debt or obligation incurred in aid of insurrection or rebellion against the United States, or any claim for the loss or emancipation of any slave; but all such debts, obligations and claims shall be held illegal and void.

Section 5.

The Congress shall have power to enforce, by appropriate legislation, the provisions of this article.

Amendment 15. Right to Vote (1870)

Passed by Congress February 26, 1869.

Ratified February 3, 1870.

Section 1.

The right of citizens of the United States to vote shall not be denied or abridged by the United States or by any state on account of race, color, or previous condition of servitude.

Section 2.

The Congress shall have power to enforce this article by appropriate legislation.

Amendment 16. Income Tax (1913)

Passed by Congress July 12, 1909.

Ratified February 3, 1913.

Note: Article 1, Section 9, of the Constitution was modified by Amendment 16.

The Congress shall have power to lay and collect taxes on incomes, from whatever source derived, without apportionment among the several states, and without regard to any census or enumeration.

Amendment 17. Direct Election of Senators (1913)

Passed by Congress May 13, 1912.

Ratified April 8, 1913.

Note: Article 1, Section 3, of the Constitution was modified by Amendment 17.

Section 1.

The Senate of the United States shall be composed of 2 Senators from each state, elected by the people thereof, for 6 years; and each Senator shall have one vote. The electors in each state shall have the qualifications requisite for electors of the most numerous branch of the state legislature.

Section 2.

When vacancies happen in the representation of any state in the Senate, the executive authority of such state shall issue writs of election to fill such vacancies: Provided, that the legislature of any state may empower the executive thereof to make temporary appointments until the people fill the vacancies by election as the legislature may direct.

Section 3.

This amendment shall not be so construed as to affect the election or term of any Senator chosen before it becomes valid as part of the Constitution.

Amendment 18. Prohibition (1919)

Passed by Congress December 18, 1917.

Ratified January 16, 1919.

Note: Repealed by the Amendment 21.

Section 1.

After one year from the ratification of this article the manufacture, sale, or transportation of intoxicating liquors within, the importation thereof into, or the

exportation thereof from the United States and all territory subject to the jurisdiction thereof for beverage purposes is hereby prohibited.

Section 2.

The Congress and the several states shall have concurrent power to enforce this article by appropriate legislation.

Section 3.

This article shall be inoperative unless it shall have been ratified as an amendment to the Constitution by the legislatures of the several states, as provided in the Constitution, within 7 years from the date of the submission hereof to the states by the Congress.

Amendment 19. Woman Suffrage (1920)

Passed by Congress June 4, 1919.

Ratified August 18, 1920

Section 1.

The right of citizens of the United States to vote shall not be denied or abridged by the United States or by any state on account of sex.

Section 2.

Congress shall have power to enforce this article by appropriate legislation.

Amendment 20, "Lame Duck" Session (1933)

Passed by Congress March 2, 1932.

Ratified January 23, 1933.

Note: Article 1, Section 4, of the Constitution was modified by Section 2 of Amendment 20. A portion of Amendment 12 was superseded by Section 3 of Amendment 20.

Section 1.

The terms of the President and Vice-President shall end at noon on the 20th day of January, and the terms of Senators and Representatives at noon on the 3rd day of January, of the years in which such terms would have ended if this article had not been ratified; and the terms of their successors shall then begin.

Section 2.

The Congress shall assemble at least once in every year, and such meeting shall begin at noon on the 3rd day of January, unless they shall by law appoint a different day.

Section 3.

If, at the time fixed for the beginning of the term of the President, the President elect shall have died, the Vice-President elect shall become President. If a President shall not have been chosen before the time fixed for the beginning of his term, or if the President elect shall have failed to qualify, then the Vice-President elect shall act as President until a President shall have qualified; and the Congress may by law provide for the case wherein neither a President elect nor a Vice-President elect shall have qualified, declaring who shall then act as President, or the manner in which one who is to act

shall be selected, and such person shall act accordingly until a President or Vice-President shall have qualified.

Section 4.

The Congress may by law provide for the case of the death of any of the persons from whom the House of Representatives may choose a President whenever the right of choice shall have devolved upon them, and for the case of death of any of the persons from whom the Senate may choose a Vice-President whenever the right of choice shall have devolved upon them.

Section 5.

Section 1 and 2 shall take effect on the 15th day of October following the ratification of this article.

Section 6. .

This article shall be inoperative unless it shall have been ratified as an amendment to the Constitution by the legislatures of ¾ of the several states within 7 years from the date of its submission.

Amendment 21. Repeal of Prohibition (1933)

Passed by Congress February 20, 1933.

Ratified December 5, 1933.

Section 1.

The 18th article of the amendment to the Constitution of the United States is hereby repealed.

Section 2.

The transportation or importation into any state,

territory, or possession of the United States for delivery or use therein of intoxicating liquors, in violation of the laws thereof, is hereby prohibited.

Section 3.

This article shall be inoperative unless it shall have been ratified as an amendment to the Constitution by conventions in the several states, as provided in the Constitution, within 7 years from the date of the submission hereof to the states by the Congress.

Amendment 22. Limit on Presidential Terms (1951)

Passed by Congress March 21, 1947.

Ratified February 27, 1951.

Section 1.

No person shall be elected to the office of the President more than twice, and no person who has held the office of President, or acted as President, for more than 2 years of a term to which some other person was elected President shall be elected to the office of the President more than once. *But this article shall not apply to any person holding the office of President when this article was proposed by the Congress, and shall not prevent any person who may be holding the office of President, or acting as President, during the term within which this article becomes operative from holding the office of President during the remainder of such term.*

Section 2.

This article shall be inoperative unless it shall have

been ratified as an amendment to the Constitution by the legislatures of ¾ of the several states within 7 years from the date of its submission to the states by the Congress.

Amendment 23. Voting in District of Columbia (1961)

Passed by Congress June 17, 1960.

Ratified March 29, 1961.

Section 1.

The district constituting the seat of the government of the United States shall appoint in such manner as Congress may direct: a number of electors of President and Vice-President equal to the whole number of Senators and Representatives in Congress to which the district would be entitled if it were a state, but in no event more than the least populous state; they shall be in addition to those appointed by the states, but they shall be considered, for the purpose of the election of President and Vice-President, to be electors appointed by a state; and they shall meet in the district and perform such duties as provided by the 12th article of amendment

Section 2.

The Congress shall have power to enforce this article by appropriate legislation.

Amendment 24. Abolition of Poll Taxes (1964)

Passed by Congress August 27, 1962.

Ratified January 23, 1964.

Section 1.

The right of citizens of the United States to vote in any primary or other election for President or Vice-President, for electors for President or Vice-President, or for Senator or Representative in Congress, shall not be denied or abridged by the United States or any state by reason of failure to pay any poll tax or other tax.

Section 2.

The Congress shall have power to enforce this article by appropriate legislation.

Amendment 25. Presidential Disability, Succession (1967)

Passed by Congress July 6, 1965.

Ratified February 10, 1967.

Note: Article 2, Section 1, of the Constitution was affected by Amendment 25.

Section 1.

In case of the removal of the President from office or of his death or resignation, the Vice-President shall become President.

Section 2.

Whenever there is a vacancy in the office of the Vice

President, the President shall nominate a Vice-President who shall take office upon confirmation by a majority vote of both houses of Congress.

Section 3.

Whenever the President transmits to the President pro tempore of the Senate and the Speaker of the House of Representatives his written declaration that he is unable to discharge the powers and duties of his office, and until he transmits to them a written declaration to the contrary, such powers and duties shall be discharged by the Vice-President as Acting President.

Section 4.

Whenever the Vice-President and a majority of either the principal officers of the executive departments or of such other body as Congress may by law provide, transmit to the President pro tempore of the Senate and the speaker of the House of Representatives their written declaration that the President is unable to discharge the powers and duties of his office, the Vice-President shall immediately assume the powers and duties of the office as Acting President. Thereafter, when the President transmits to the President pro tempore of the Senate and the Speaker of the House of Representatives his written declaration that no inability exists, he shall resume the powers and duties of his office unless the Vice-President and a majority of either the principal officers of the executive department(s) or of such other body as Congress may by law provide, transmit within 4 days to the President pro tempore of the Senate and the Speaker of the House of Representatives their

USA FACTBOOK

written declaration that the President is unable to discharge the powers and duties of his office. Thereupon Congress shall decide the issue, assembling within 48 hours for that purpose if not in session. If the Congress, within 21 days after receipt of the latter written declaration, or, if Congress is not in session, within 21 days after Congress is required to assemble, determines by 2/3 vote of both houses that the President is unable to discharge the powers and duties of his office, the Vice-President shall continue to discharge the same as Acting President; otherwise, the President shall resume the powers and duties of his office.

Amendment 26. 18 – year – old Vote (1971)

Passed by Congress March 23, 1971.

Ratified July 1, 1971.

Note: Amendment 14, Section 2, of the Constitution was modified by Section 1 of Amendment 26.

Section 1.

The right of citizens of the United States, who are 18 years of age or older, to vote shall not be denied or abridged by the United States or by any state on account of age.

Section 2.

The Congress shall have power to enforce this article by appropriate legislation.

Amendment 27. Congressional Pay (1992)

Passed by Congress September 25, 1789.

Ratified May 7, 1992.

No law, varying the compensation for services of the Senators and Representatives, shall take effect, until an election of Representatives shall have intervened.

WARS

REVOLUTIONARY WAR

Years – 1775 to 1783

Battle Deaths – 4,435

Non–Mortal Woundings – 6,188

WAR OF 1812

Years – 1812 to 1815

Battle Deaths – 2,260

Non–Mortal Woundings – 4,505

MEXICAN – AMERICAN WAR

Years – 1846 to 1848

Battle Deaths – 1,733

Other Deaths in Service – 11,550

Non–Mortal Woundings – 4,152

CIVIL WAR

Years – 1861 to 1865

Union

Battle Deaths –140,414

Other Deaths in Service – 224,097

Non–Mortal Woundings – 281,881

Confederate

Battle Deaths – 74, 524

Other Deaths in Service – 59,297

Non–Mortal Woundings – unknown

SPANISH–AMERICAN WAR

Years – 1898 to 1902

Battle Deaths – 385

Other Deaths in Service – 2,061

Non–Mortal Woundings – 1,662

PHILIPPINE–AMERICAN WAR

Years – 1899 to1901

Battle Deaths – 1,108

Non–Mortal Woundings – 2,779

WORLD WAR I

Years – 1917 to 1918

Battle Deaths – 53,402

Other Deaths in Service – 63,114

Non–Mortal Woundings – 204,002

WORLD WAR II

Years – 1940 to 1945

Battle Deaths – 291,557

Other Deaths in Service – 113,842

Non–Mortal Woundings – 671,846

KOREAN WAR

Years – 1950 to 1953

Battle Deaths – 33,686

Other Deaths – 2,830

Other Deaths in Service – 17,730

Non–Mortal Woundings – 103,284

Vietnam War

Years – 1964 to 1975

Battle Deaths – 47,410

Other Deaths – 10,788

Other Deaths in Service – 32,000 est.

Non–Mortal Woundings – 153,303

Gulf War

Years – 1990 to 1991

Battle Deaths – 148

Other Deaths – 235

Other Deaths in Service – 914

Non–Mortal Woundings – 467

War Against Terrorism

Years – 2001 to _____

Battle Deaths – _____

Other Deaths – _____

Other Deaths in Service – _____

Non - Mortal Woundings – _____

WAR IN IRAQ (IRAQI FREEDOM)

Years – 2003 to _____

Battle Deaths – _____

Other Deaths – _____

Other Deaths in Service – _____

Non–Mortal Woundings – _____

Years – _____

Battle Deaths – _____

Other Deaths – _____

Other Deaths in Service – _____

Non–Mortal Woundings – _____

PATRIOTIC SONGS

PLEDGE OF ALLEGIANCE

I pledge allegiance to the flag of the United States of America and to the Republic for which it stands. One nation under God, indivisible with liberty and justice for all.

GOD BLESS AMERICA

God Bless America
Land that I love
Stand Beside her and guide her
Thru the night with a light from above

From the mountains to the prairies
To the oceans white with foam
God Bless America
My home sweet home

MY COUNTRY, `TIS OF THEE

My country `tis of thee,
Sweet land of liberty,
Of thee I sing.

Land where my fathers died,
Land of the Pilgrims' pride,
From every mountainside,
Let freedom ring.

Our fathers' God, to thee,
Author of liberty,

To thee we sing.
Long may our land be bright,
With freedom's holy light;
Protect us by thy might,
Great God, our King!

AMERICA THE BEAUTIFUL

Oh beautiful for spacious skies,
For amber waves of grain,
For purple mountain majesties,
Above the fruited plain.
America! America!
God shed His grace on thee,
And crown thy good with brotherhood,
From sea to shining sea.

Oh beautiful for pilgrim feet,
Whose stern impassioned stress.
A thoroughfare of freedom beat,
Across the wilderness.
America! America!
God mend thine ev'ry flaw,
Confirm thy soul in self-control,
Thy liberty in law.

Oh beautiful for heroes proved in liberating strife,
Who more than self their country loved, and mercy
more than life,
America! America! May God thy gold refine,
Till all success be nobleness,
And ev'ry gain divine.

Oh beautiful for patriot dream
That sees beyond the years.
Thine alabaster cities gleam
Undimmed by human tears.
America! America!
God shed his grace on thee,
And crown thy good with brotherhood
From sea to shining sea.

THE STAR–SPANGLED BANNER

Oh, say can you see,
By the dawn's early light,
What so proudly we hailed at the twilight's last
gleaming?
Whose broad stripes and bright stars, through the per-
ilous fight,
O'er the ramparts we watched, were so gallantly
streaming?

And the rocket's red glare, the bombs bursting in air,
Gave proof through the night that our flag was still
there.
O say does that star - spangled banner yet wave.
O'er the land of the free and the home of the brave?

On the shore, dimly seen through the mists of the
deep,
Where the foe's haughty host in dread silence reposes,
What is that which the breeze, o'er the towering steep,
As it fitfully blows, now conceals, now discloses?

Now it catches the gleam of the morning's first beam,

in full glory reflected now shines on the stream:
`Tis the star - spangled banner!
O long may it wave
O'er the land of the free and the home of the brave.

And where is that band who so vauntingly swore
That the havoc of war and the battle's confusion
A home and a country should leave us no more?
Their blood has wiped out their foul footstep's pollu-
tion.

No refuge could save the hirling and slave
From the terror of flight, or the gloom of the grave:
And the star - spangled banner in triumph doth wave
O'er the land of the free and the home of the brave.

Oh! Thus be it ever, when freemen shall stand
Between their loved homes and the war's desolation!
Blest with victory and peace, may the heaven- rescued
land
Praise the Power that hath made and preserved us a
nation.

Then conquer we must, for our cause it is just,
And this be our motto:
"In God is our trust."
And the star- spangled banner forever shall wave
O'er the land of the free and the home of the brave!

About The Author

Christopher L. Hickman was born and raised in Michigan City, Indiana and lists professional basketball and baseball among his favorite pastimes.

Books he has enjoyed reading are The Holy Bible, The Holy Quran, books on Buddhism and nearly all books on American history and culture.

This book was assembled to help citizens, children and immigrants get basic information of the USA easily and effectively.

Christopher splits his time between Milwaukee, Wisconsin and Michigan City where he lives and works.

www.ingramcontent.com/pod-product-compliance
Lightning Source LLC
Chambersburg PA
CBHW021106090426
42738CB00006B/523